Use the secret code to answer the riddle.

What game do you win by going backwards?

____ ____ ____   ____ ____   ____ ____ ____

Secret Code

= a	= f	= g	= o
= r	= t	= u	= w

Use the word list to solve the crossword puzzle.

Across

4. Bears have sharp ____.
6. Bears sleep, or ____, all winter.
8. A large grayish bear found in North America is a ____.

Down

1. A wooded place where bears live is a ____.
2. A bear might make its home in a ____.
3. Baby bears are called ____.
5. A ____ is a noise a bear makes.
7. A toy bear with stuffing inside is called a ____ bear.

Word List

growl

cave

forest

claws

hibernate

grizzly

cubs

teddy

Use the secret code to answer the riddle.

What pierces ears without making any holes?

Secret Code

✚ = a   △ = d   ▼ = e   ☆ = i   ▢ = l

人 = n   ✖ = o   ⬡ = s   ● = u

3

Use the word list to solve the crossword puzzle.

Word List

lonely
proud
surprised
angry
bored
sad
happy
afraid

Across

2. You may be _____ when you don't get your way.
5. Be _____ of a job well done.
6. The boy was _____ when he opened the gift.
7. Doing the same thing over and over can make a person _____.

Down

1. Don't be _____ of the dark.
3. When you are all by yourself, you may feel _____.
4. I'm so _____ we are going on vacation.
6. I could tell by the _____ look on the boy's face that he was unhappy.

4

Use the secret code to answer the riddle.

What has lots of ears but cannot hear?

$\overline{}_{93}$ $\overline{}_{65}$ $\overline{}_{52}$ $\overline{}_{25}$ $\overline{}_{56}$ $\overline{}_{47}$ $\overline{}_{12}$ $\overline{}_{39}$ $\overline{}_{74}$ $\overline{}_{21}$

Secret Code

93 = a   65 = c   21 = d   39 = e   47 = f

12 = i   74 = l   56 = n   52 = o   25 = r

Use the word list to solve the crossword puzzle.

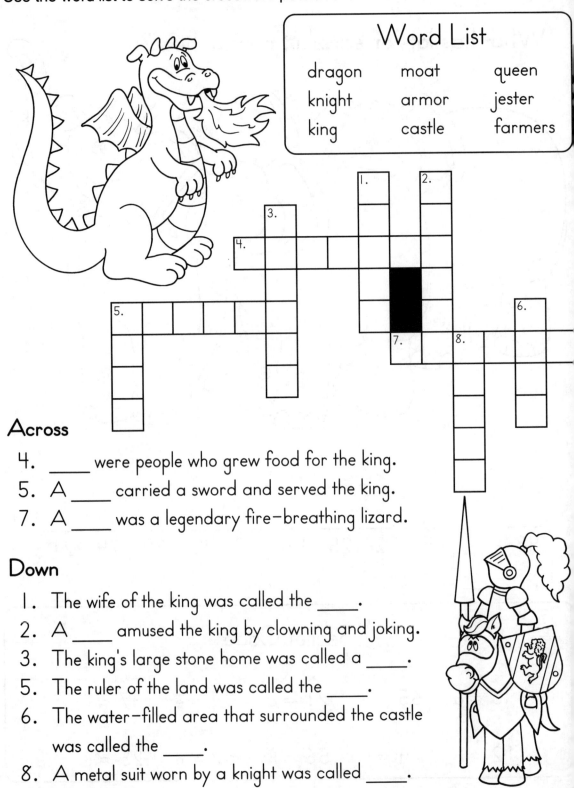

Word List

dragon	moat	queen
knight	armor	jester
king	castle	farmers

Across

4. ____ were people who grew food for the king.
5. A ____ carried a sword and served the king.
7. A ____ was a legendary fire-breathing lizard.

Down

1. The wife of the king was called the ____.
2. A ____ amused the king by clowning and joking.
3. The king's large stone home was called a ____.
5. The ruler of the land was called the ____.
6. The water-filled area that surrounded the castle was called the ____.
8. A metal suit worn by a knight was called ____.

Use the secret code to answer the riddle.

What building has the most stories?

___   ___ ___ ___ ___ ___ ___ ___

Secret Code

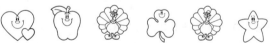

= a   = b   = i

= l   = r   = y

Use the word list to solve the crossword puzzle.

Word List

trees	insect	seasons	animal
storm	seed	weather	blossom

Across

2. A tiny animal with six legs is an ____.
3. A flower on a tree is called a ____.
6. The ____ report will help you know how to dress each morning.
7. When you hear thunder there's usually a ____ coming.
8. A tiny object from which a plant grows is a ____.

Down

1. A bird is an ____.
4. Winter, spring, summer, and fall are all ____.
5. There are many ____ in the forest.

Use the secret code to answer the riddle.

What has two hands but never holds anything?

<u> </u>   <u> </u> <u> </u> <u> </u> <u> </u> <u> </u>
   ★ ☐ ★ ★ ●

Secret Code

✛ = a   ★ = c   ● = k   ☐ = l   ★ = o

Use the word list to solve the crossword puzzle.

Word List

classroom	homework	study	student
books	teacher	learn	desk

Across

1. To make good grades, you have to _____ hard.
4. The place at school where a group of students learn together is a
   _____.
5. Students sit at a _____ to write.
6. We _____ many things at school.
7. Pages with words and pictures can be found in _____.

Down

2. A person who helps us to learn is a _____.
3. Studying that is done after school is called _____.
8. A child who goes to school is a _____.

Use the secret code to answer the riddle.

What kind of driver doesn't need a license?

a __ __ __ __ __ __ __ __ __ __ __
  4   1   7   9   8   5   7   6   3   9   7

Secret Code

1 = c	5 = d	9 = e	6 = i
7 = r	4 = s	3 = v	8 = w

Use the word list to solve the crossword puzzle.

Across

2. Baby birds ____ from eggs.
5. Water and ____ are necessary to grow things.
6. Flowers ____ in spring.
7. Lots of ____ occurs in the springtime.

Down

1. During spring, seeds sprout and ____ begin to grow.
3. Windy days are great for flying a ____.
4. The ____ between winter and summer is spring.
5. April ____ bring May flowers.

Word List

hatch

season

kite

plants

growth

sunshine

showers

bloom

Use the secret code to answer the riddle.

How do you talk to a giant?

___ ___ ___ ___ ___ ___ ___ ___ ___ ___ ___

Secret Code

= b   = d   = e   = g

= i   = o   = r   = s

= u   = w

13

Use the word list to solve the crossword puzzle.

Word List

skating

frozen

hockey

bobsled

shovel

snowshoes

skiing

snowballs

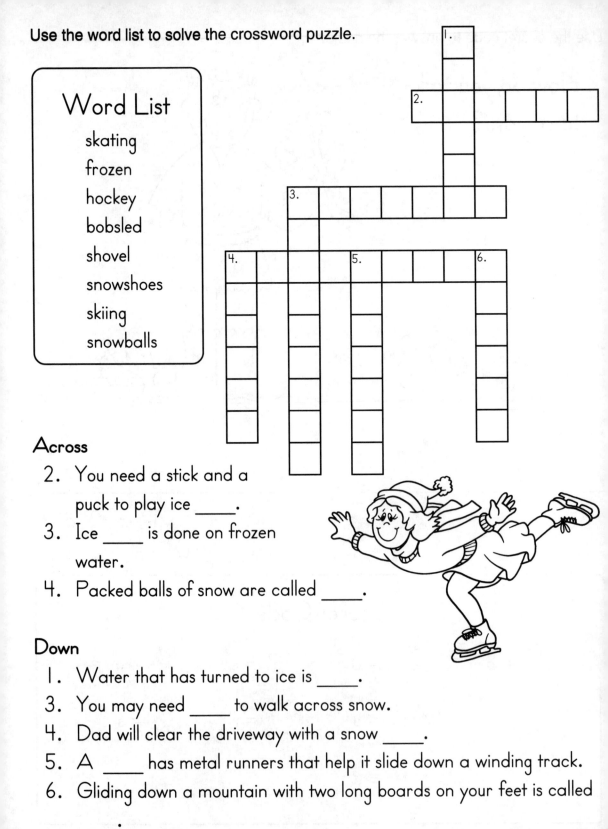

Across

2. You need a stick and a puck to play ice ____.
3. Ice ____ is done on frozen water.
4. Packed balls of snow are called ____.

Down

1. Water that has turned to ice is ____.
3. You may need ____ to walk across snow.
4. Dad will clear the driveway with a snow ____.
5. A ____ has metal runners that help it slide down a winding track.
6. Gliding down a mountain with two long boards on your feet is called ____.

Use the secret code to answer the riddle.

What do you drop when you need it and take back when you don't?

 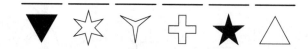

Secret Code

▼ = a   Y = c   ✚ = h

☆ = n   ★ = o   △ = r

Use the word list to solve the crossword puzzle.

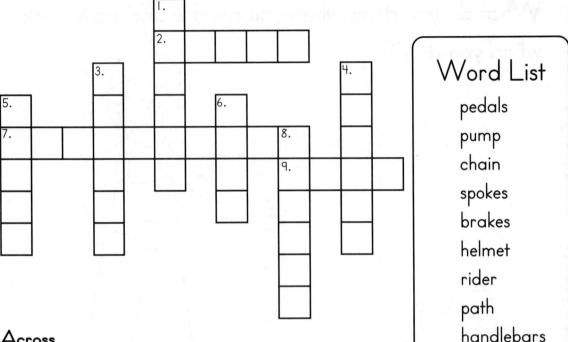

Word List

pedals
pump
chain
spokes
brakes
helmet
rider
path
handlebars

Across

2. A person who sits on a bike while it moves is the ____.
7. Always keep both hands on the ____.
9. You need a ____ to put air in your tires.

Down

1. Applying the ____ will stop a bike.
3. On a bike, your feet go on the ____.
4. A bike rider should wear a ____.
5. The ____ helps turn the wheel.
6. A trail for bike riding is also called a ____.
8. The ____ are part of the wheel.

Use the secret code to answer the riddle.

What do zebras have that no other animals have?

<u>   </u> <u>   </u> <u>   </u> <u>   </u>　　<u>   </u> <u>   </u> <u>   </u> <u>   </u> <u>   </u> <u>   </u>

71 14 71 12   17 11 71 16 14 21

Secret Code

14 = a	71 = b	11 = e	21 = s
16 = r	12 = y	17 = z	

Use the word list to solve the crossword puzzle.

Word List

job

paycheck

worker

occupation

desk

telephone

office

computer

salary

Across

2. Your ____ is what you do for a living.

8. A piece of furniture where you sit down to work is a ____.

9. A ____ helps us talk to others who aren't in the same room.

Down

1. A ____ is what one is paid for the work they do.

3. A machine that helps us do work is a ____.

4. My father wears a suit when he goes to his ____ to work.

5. Every Friday, most workers get a _____.

6. A person who gets the job done is a ____.

7. Another name for work is a ____.

Use the secret code to answer the riddle.

What does a farmer grow if he works day and night?

___ ___   ___ ___ ___ ___ ___   ___ ___ ___ ___ ___

Secret Code

 = d   = e   = g   = h   = i

 = o   = r   = s   = t   = w

19

Use the word list to solve the crossword puzzle.

Word List
- clothing
- jacket
- socks
- jewelry
- dress
- belt
- pants
- shoes
- mittens

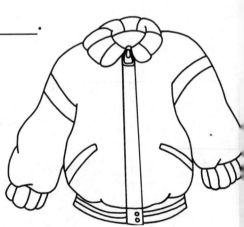

Across
2. When it's cold, wear a ____.
5. Our ____ covers our bodies and keeps us warm.
6. Put your ____ on before your shoes.
8. I like to look at my mother's wedding ____.

Down
1. A ____ helps to hold up pants.
2. Rings and bracelets are called ____.
3. Put on your ____ before making a snowball.
4. We wear ____ to cover our legs.
7. Put on your socks and then your ___.

Use the secret code to answer the riddle.

What stays hot even in the refrigerator?

Secret Code

✛ = a   ⬠ = d   ⬡ = h   ● = m   ▽ = o

⅄ = r   ★ = s   △ = t   Y = u

21

Use the word list to solve the crossword puzzle.

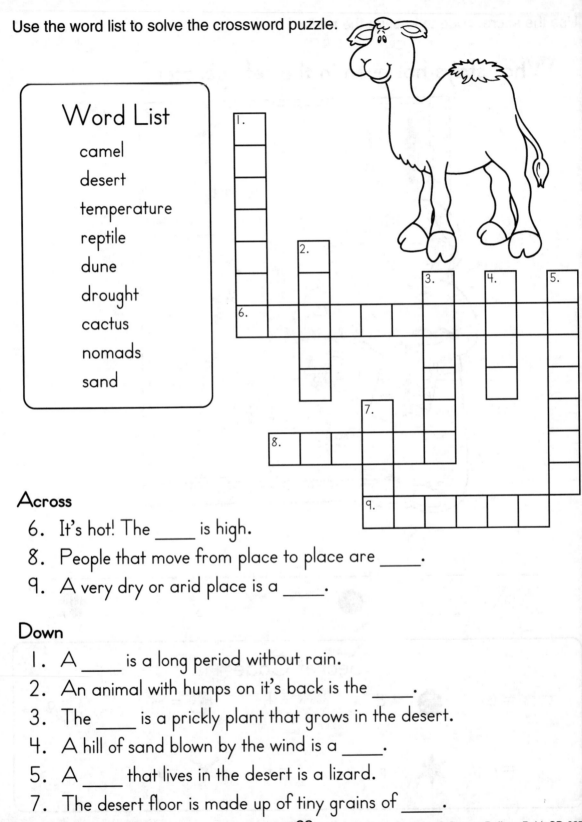

Word List

camel

desert

temperature

reptile

dune

drought

cactus

nomads

sand

Across

6. It's hot! The _____ is high.

8. People that move from place to place are _____.

9. A very dry or arid place is a _____.

Down

1. A _____ is a long period without rain.

2. An animal with humps on it's back is the _____.

3. The _____ is a prickly plant that grows in the desert.

4. A hill of sand blown by the wind is a _____.

5. A _____ that lives in the desert is a lizard.

7. The desert floor is made up of tiny grains of _____.

Use the secret code to answer the riddle.

How did the elephant get to the top of the tree?

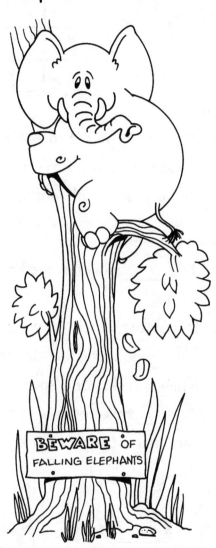

$\overline{45}\ \overline{30}$ $\overline{49}\ \overline{9}\ \overline{20}$

$\overline{15}\ \overline{81}$ $\overline{9}\ \overline{81}$

$\overline{9}\ \overline{64}\ \overline{15}\ \overline{25}\ \overline{81}$

$\overline{9}\ \overline{81}\ \overline{72}$

$\overline{36}\ \overline{9}\ \overline{4}\ \overline{20}\ \overline{30}\ \overline{72}$

Secret Code

9 = a	64 = c	72 = d	30 = e
45 = h	4 = i	81 = n	15 = o
25 = r	49 = s	20 = t	36 = w

Use the word list to solve the crossword puzzle.

Across

5. A place to go out to eat is a ____.
8. Chocolate cake is my favorite ____.
9. Wipe your mouth with a ____.

Down

1. The ____ works in the kitchen preparing meals.
2. Breakfast, lunch, and dinner are all ____.
3. I like ranch dressing on my ____.
4. Knives, forks, and spoons are all ____.
6. A ____ takes orders in a restaurant.
7. Another word for drink is ____.

Word List

dessert
waiter
meals
chef
restaurant
salad
napkin
beverage
utensils

Use the secret code to answer the riddle.

What can be seen in the water but is not wet?

A R e f l e c t i o n

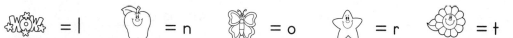

Secret Code

☺ = a	= c	✓ = e	= f	= i
WOW = l	= n	= o	= r	= t

Use the word list to solve the crossword puzzle.

Word List

children

games

neighbor

share

family

like

friend

play

secret

Down

1. Something that you don't want others to know is a _____.
2. It's nice to _____ our toys.
4. We played many _____ at the party.
5. I like to _____ outside until dinner time.
7. Someone that you like to play with is a _____.
8. Friends usually _____ each other.

Across

3. The person who lives near you is your _____.
6. Another name for kids is _____.
7. The members of a household are called a _____.

Use the secret code to answer the riddle.

What has four wheels and flies?

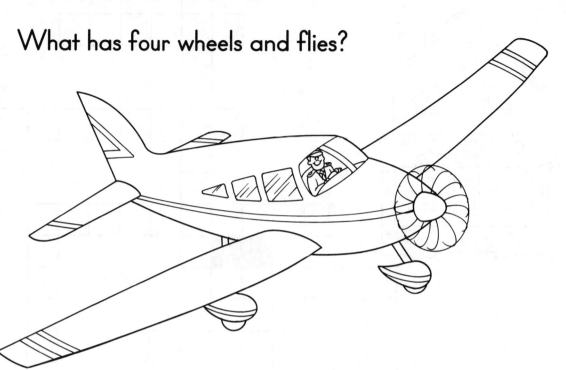

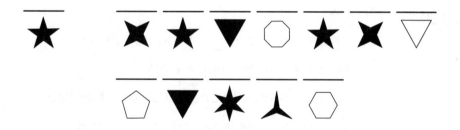

Use the word list to solve the crossword puzzle.

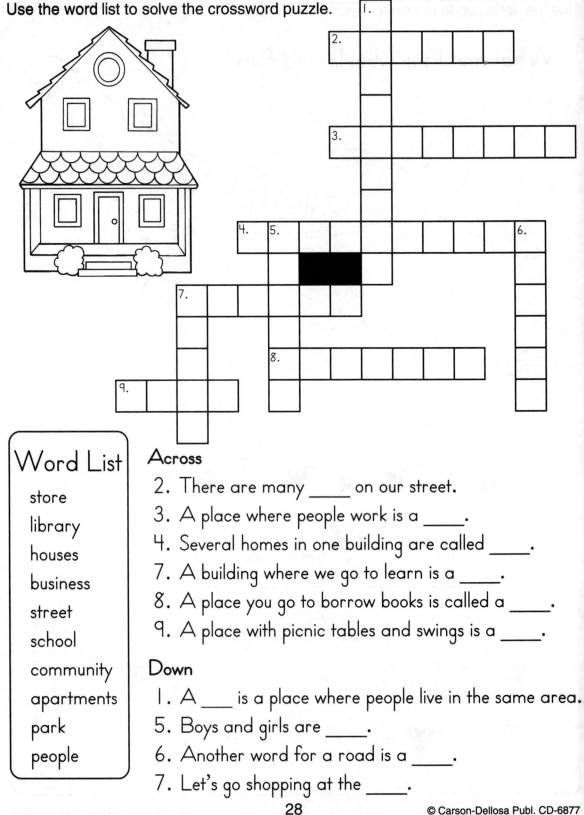

Word List
- store
- library
- houses
- business
- street
- school
- community
- apartments
- park
- people

Across
2. There are many ____ on our street.
3. A place where people work is a ____.
4. Several homes in one building are called ____.
7. A building where we go to learn is a ____.
8. A place you go to borrow books is called a ____.
9. A place with picnic tables and swings is a ____.

Down
1. A ___ is a place where people live in the same area.
5. Boys and girls are ____.
6. Another word for a road is a ____.
7. Let's go shopping at the ____.

28

Use the secret code to answer the riddle.

When does your skeleton laugh?

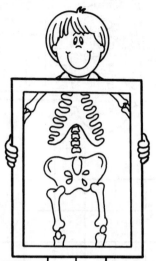
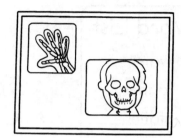

___ ___ ___ ___   ___ ___ ___ ___ ___ ___ ___
4   6   10   1   3   16   14   10   16   1   10

___ ___ ___ ___ ___ ___ ___   ___ ___ ___ ___
15   12   8   11   2   10   3   13   16   7   24

___ ___ ___ ___ ___   ___ ___ ___ ___
9   7   1   1   13   5   16   1   10

Secret Code

5 = b	8 = c	10 = e	9 = f	6 = h
12 = i	11 = k	2 = l	14 = m	1 = n
16 = o	24 = r	3 = s	15 = t	7 = u
4 = w	13 = y			

Use the word list to solve the crossword puzzle.

Word List

- water
- ladder
- station
- hydrant
- truck
- hose
- firefighter
- siren
- alarm
- flames

Across

2. Firetrucks are parked at the _____ when not in use.

3. A person who puts out fires is a _____.

5. Fire hoses spray _____ on a fire to put it out.

6. Firefighters climb a _____ to get to the top of a building.

7. A smoke detector is a type of _____.

8. A _____ warns people that a fire truck is on the road.

9. A firefighter rides on a fire _____ to get to the fire.

Down

1. Water comes out of the firefighters' _____ in a powerful stream.

3. When a building is on fire, you will see black smoke and red _____.

4. Firefighters get water from a _____.

30

Use the secret code to answer the riddle.

What is the name of the place that fortune tellers go to dance?

the crystal

ball

Secret Code

▽ = a	✚ = b	⬣ = c	⬠ = d	⬡ = e
■ = f	Y = g	△ = h	⅄ = i	▼ = j
★ = k	□ = l	⊹ = m	⬠ = n	● = o
⋏ = p	⬭ = q	▲ = r	✦ = s	Y = t
☆ = u	✬ = v	★ = w	☆ = x	○ = y
⬣ = z				

Use the word list to solve the crossword puzzle.

Word List

hail	clouds
sunshine	fog
rain	storm
wind	thunder
tornado	blizzard

Across

2. The _____ feels warm.
3. Wind, along with rain, thunder, and lightning is usually called a _____.
6. It's snowing so hard I can't see. This is called a _____.
8. Water falling from the sky is _____.
9. March is a month of strong _____.
10. A cloud near the ground that is hard to see through is called _____.

Down

1. Boom! It must be _____.
4. A funnel of wind is called a _____.
5. Before a storm, you usually see many _____.
7. Rain in the form of small frozen pellets is _____.

32

Use the secret code to answer the riddle.

Who earns a living without doing a day's work?

$$\underline{}_{3} \qquad \underline{}_{5} \; \underline{}_{16} \; \underline{}_{8} \; \underline{}_{13} \; \underline{}_{23}$$

$$\underline{}_{24} \; \underline{}_{3} \; \underline{}_{23} \; \underline{}_{20} \; \underline{}_{13} \; \underline{}_{25} \; \underline{}_{3} \; \underline{}_{5}$$

Secret Code

3 = a	15 = b	20 = c	2 = d	6 = e
22 = f	8 = g	13 = h	16 = i	18 = j
10 = k	17 = l	25 = m	5 = n	11 = o
26 = p	21 = q	1 = r	14 = s	23 = t
4 = u	7 = v	24 = w	9 = x	19 = y
12 = z				

Use the word list to solve the crossword puzzle.

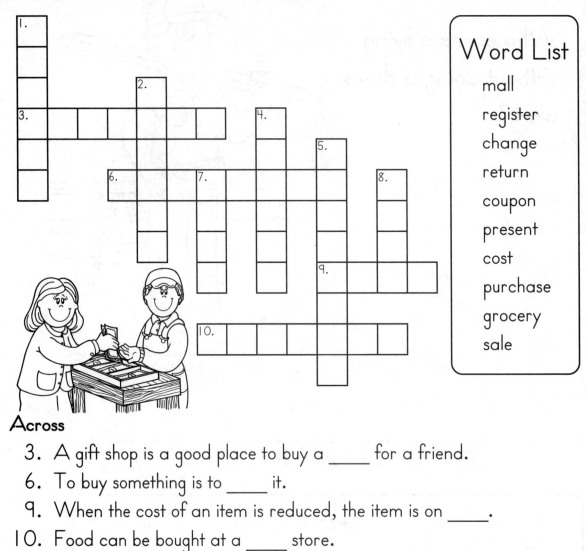

Word List

mall

register

change

return

coupon

present

cost

purchase

grocery

sale

Across

3. A gift shop is a good place to buy a _____ for a friend.
6. To buy something is to _____ it.
9. When the cost of an item is reduced, the item is on _____.
10. Food can be bought at a _____ store.

Down

1. A slip of paper that reduces the price of an item is called a _____.
2. You can get your money back from a purchase if you _____ what you bought.
4. When you pay too much for an item, you will receive _____.
5. The cash _____ is where you pay for merchandise.
7. The _____ of an item is its price.
8. A building that contains many different shops is called a _____.

Use the secret code to answer the riddle.

What runs around the yard but never moves?

Secret Code

□ = a	★ = b	⬣ = c	⬠ = d	⬡ = e
■ = f	Y = g	△ = h	▲ = i	◯ = j
☆ = k	▽ = l	✚ = m	⬠ = n	● = o
⬥ = p	⬡ = q	⬡ = r	✖ = s	Y = t
⬠ = u	✶ = v	▼ = w	✚ = x	★ = y
⬥ = z				

Use the word list to solve the crossword puzzle.

Word List

- pool
- water
- goggles
- raft
- ocean
- bubbles
- kick
- dive
- stroke
- splash

Across

2. Swimmers use their legs to ____.
4. A person wears ___ over his eyes to help him see underwater.
7. Air ____ float to the surface of the water.
9. A ____ can be used to ride on the waves.
10. The large body of water at the beach is called the ____.

Down

1. You ____ into the water when you jump head first.
3. A large container with water for swimming is called a ____.
5. A swimmer's arm motion is called a ____.
6. Don't dive into a pool if you don't know the depth of the ____.
8. Jumping into water will cause a ____.

36

Use the secret code to answer the riddle.

What goes up when you count down?

$\overline{}$ $\overline{}$ $\overline{}$ $\overline{}$ $\overline{}$ $\overline{}$ $\overline{}$
  4   8   50   18   24   28   14

Secret Code

4 = a	38 = b	18 = c	10 = d	28 = e
36 = f	2 = g	26 = h	48 = i	42 = j
24 = k	44 = l	34 = m	22 = n	50 = o
40 = p	32 = q	8 = r	46 = s	14 = t
6 = u	16 = v	12 = w	30 = x	52 = y
20 = z				

Use the word list to solve the crossword puzzle.

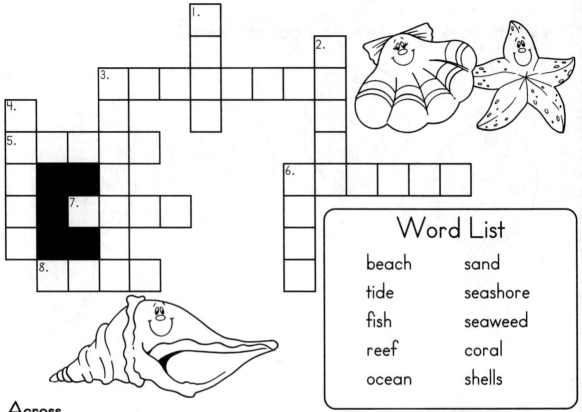

Word List

beach	sand
tide	seashore
fish	seaweed
reef	coral
ocean	shells

Across

3. Another name for the coast is the ____.
5. A marine animal that looks like colorful rock is ____.
6. Many people like to walk along the beach and collect ____.
7. A ____ is a ridge of rock or coral near the surface of the water.
8. The rise and fall of the sea is called the ____.

Down

1. Many different types of ____ swim in the sea.
2. A ____ is covered with sand.
3. A plant that grows in the ocean is ____.
4. A large body of salty water is called an ____.
6. The beach is made of tiny grains of rock called ____.

Use the secret code to answer the riddle.

What kind of stone gets smaller the longer you hold it?

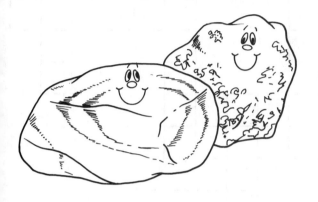

 ___

Secret Code

☆ = a	= b	Y = c	▽ = d	■ = e
= f	⬡ = g	△ = h	= i	= j
✛ = k	□ = l	○ = m	⬠ = n	★ = o
= p	▼ = q	= r	= s	= t
= u	✚ = v	★ = w	● = x	⬡ = y
▲ = z				

Use the word list to solve the crossword puzzle.

Word List

squeak   rodent
furry   tail
hide   nest
barn   cheese
whiskers   seeds

Across

3. The noise a mouse makes is called a ___.
5. The long hairs on a mouse's nose are its ___.
8. A mouse has a long ___.
9. A mouse is a type of ___.

Down

1. A ___ is a building on a farm that often has mice living in it.
2. Mice love to eat ___.
3. Mice love to eat sunflower ___.
4. A mouse will use rags and straw to make a ___.
6. Mice are hard to catch because they run and ___.
7. A mouse's coat is soft and ___.

Use the secret code to answer the riddle.

What does an anteater like on his pizza?

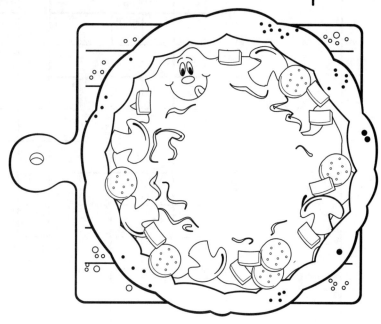

__ __ __ - __ __ __ __ __ __ __
3   31   35   7   33   19   45   47   25   9

Secret Code

3 = a	21 = b	7 = c	15 = d	25 = e
41 = f	1 = g	33 = h	47 = i	49 = j
27 = k	39 = l	29 = m	31 = n	19 = o
5 = p	13 = q	51 = r	9 = s	35 = t
37 = u	45 = v	17 = w	43 = x	11 = y
23 = z				

Use the word list to solve the crossword puzzle.

Word List

custom

vacation

festival

sharing

cards

celebrate

event

thanks

gifts

party

Across

3. Holidays are a time to ___.
4. Another word for **tradition** is ___.
5. Holidays are a time that many people send greeting ___.
6. Children enjoy unwrapping ___.
8. Everyone is invited to the ___.
10. An ___ is a special or important time.

Down

1. A day of feasting and celebration is called a ___.
2. Students get a ___ from school during the holidays.
7. Everyone enjoys ___ food and fun with family and friends.
9. People give ___ for all of the special things they have.

Use the secret code to answer the riddle.

What snack do monkeys have with their milk?

__ __ __ __ __ __ __ __ __ __

__ __ __ __ __

__ __ __ __ __ __ __

Secret Code

▽ = a	✚ = b	⬣ = c	⬠ = d	⬡ = e
■ = f	Y = g	△ = h	⊥ = i	▼ = j
★ = k	□ = l	✚ = m	⬠ = n	● = o
⋏ = p	⬣ = q	▲ = r	✦ = s	Y = t
✩ = u	✬ = v	★ = w	☆ = x	○ = y
⬣ = z				

Use the word list to solve the crossword puzzle.

Word List

lunch

grill

snack

fruit

vegetable

breakfast

meat

frozen

canned

dairy

oven

Across

3. When you cook something on a barbecue, you ___ it.
4. The first meal of the day is called ___.
7. Food that is baked is put in an ___.
8. When food is sealed in a metal container, it is ___.
10. Hamburger is a type of ___.
11. The meal that is eaten at noon is called ___.

Down

1. The freezer keeps food ___.
2. Broccoli is a ___.
5. An apple is a ___.
6. Food eaten between meals is called a ___.
9. Milk and cheese are examples of ___ foods.

44

Use the secret code to answer the riddle.

What insects like to skindive?

$\overline{}$ $\overline{}$ $\overline{}$ $\overline{}$ $\overline{}$ $\overline{}$ $\overline{}$ $\overline{}$ $\overline{}$ $\overline{}$
120 40   25   75   15 115 130 40 125 25

Secret Code

20 = a	85 = b	65 = c	10 = d	125 = e
80 = f	5 = g	35 = h	115 = i	105 = j
45 = k	60 = l	120 = m	70 = n	40 = o
95 = p	75 = q	50 = r	25 = s	130 = t
15 = u	30 = v	100 = w	90 = x	110 = y
55 = z				

Use the word list to solve the crossword puzzle.

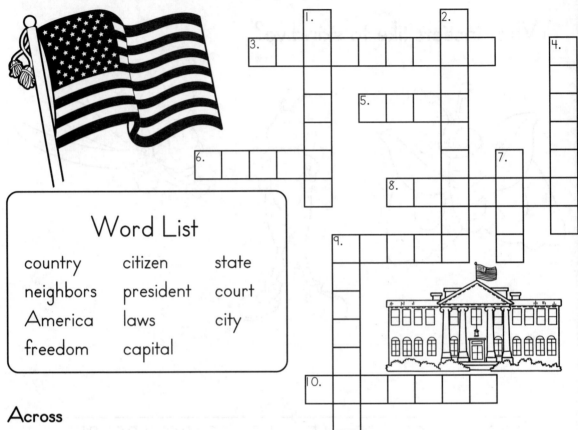

Word List

country	citizen	state
neighbors	president	court
America	laws	city
freedom	capital	

Across

3. People who live near you are your ___.
5. Rules that all citizens must follow are called ___.
6. Each star on the U.S. flag represents one ___.
8. U.S.A. stands for the United States of ___.
9. A judge hears trials in a ___.
10. Personal ___ means that citizens can make their own decisions.

Down

1. A person born in the U.S. is called a ___ of the country.
2. The chief executive of the U.S. is the ___.
4. The city that is the center of government is the ___.
7. A population center within a state is called a ___.
9. Another name for a nation is ___.

46

Use the secret code to answer the riddle.

How are a bloodhound and a rose alike?

Secret Code

▽ = a	✚ = b	⬡ = c	⬟ = d	⬡ = e
■ = f	Y = g	△ = h	⅄ = i	▼ = j
★ = k	□ = l	✛ = m	⬠ = n	● = o
⅄ = p	⬡ = q	▲ = r	✖ = s	Y = t
☆ = u	✬ = v	★ = w	☆ = x	○ = y
⬣ = z				

Use the word list to solve the crossword puzzle.

Word List

tune	sound	note
sing	dancing	radio
song	cassette	instrument
record	chorus	

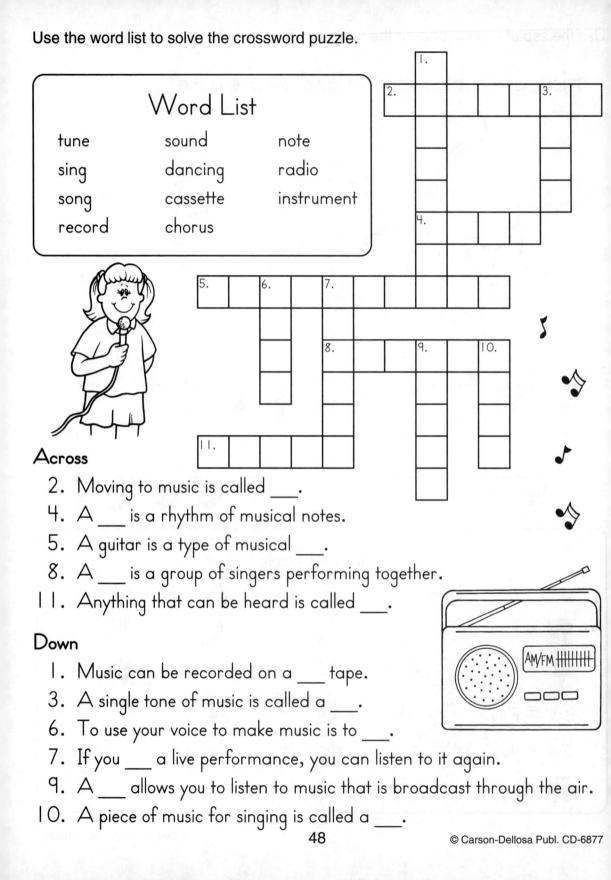

Across

2. Moving to music is called ___.
4. A ___ is a rhythm of musical notes.
5. A guitar is a type of musical ___.
8. A ___ is a group of singers performing together.
11. Anything that can be heard is called ___.

Down

1. Music can be recorded on a ___ tape.
3. A single tone of music is called a ___.
6. To use your voice to make music is to ___.
7. If you ___ a live performance, you can listen to it again.
9. A ___ allows you to listen to music that is broadcast through the air.
10. A piece of music for singing is called a ___.

Use the secret code to answer the riddle.

What do you call a small hot dog?

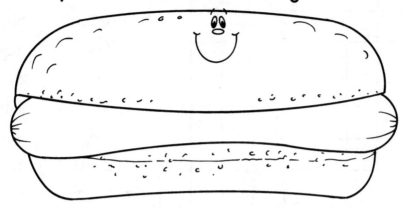

$\overline{}$ $\quad$ $\overline{}$ $\overline{}$ $\overline{}$ $\overline{}$ $\overline{}$
56 $\qquad$ 19 33 33 47 93

$\overline{}$ $\overline{}$ $\overline{}$ $\overline{}$ $\overline{}$ $\overline{}$
86 33 33 47 59 33

Secret Code

56 = a	40 = b	24 = c	85 = d	33 = e
35 = f	66 = g	13 = h	59 = i	72 = j
12 = k	51 = l	79 = m	47 = n	97 = o
76 = p	60 = q	26 = r	65 = s	19 = t
42 = u	38 = v	86 = w	83 = x	93 = y
29 = z				

Use the word list to solve the crossword puzzle.

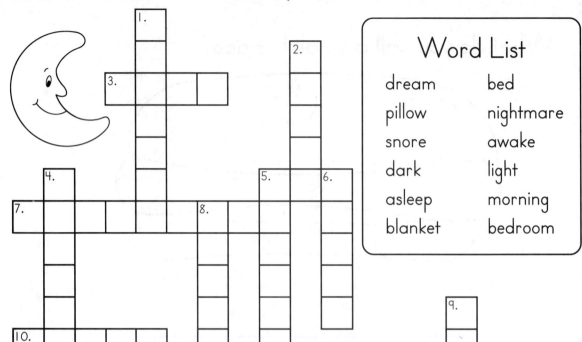

Word List

dream   bed

pillow   nightmare

snore   awake

dark   light

asleep   morning

blanket   bedroom

Across

3. When you turn off the lights, your room gets ___.
5. A ___ is a piece of furniture for sleeping.
7. A bad dream is called a ___.
10. If a person is not asleep, then he is ___.
11. The time of day that follows night is ___.

Down

1. A ___ will keep your body warm when you are in your bed.
2. Some people make a loud noise or ___ when they sleep.
4. When a person gets in bed, she puts her head on a ___.
5. The place in the house where a person sleeps is called the ___.
6. A ___ is something a person has when he is asleep.
8. Some people have a hard time falling ___.
9. A window shade will keep the ___ out of your room.

50

Use the secret code to answer the riddle.

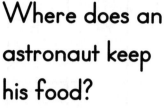

Where does an astronaut keep his food?

Secret Code

⋏ = a	☆ = b	Y = c	⬟ = d	☆ = e
■ = f	● = g	⬢ = h	◯ = i	▼ = j
△ = k	▽ = l	✚ = m	⬡ = n	Y = o
✚ = p	◯ = q	▲ = r	✗ = s	⬠ = t
✖ = u	☐ = v	★ = w	✦ = x	⋎ = y
⬣ = z				

Use the word list to solve the crossword puzzle.

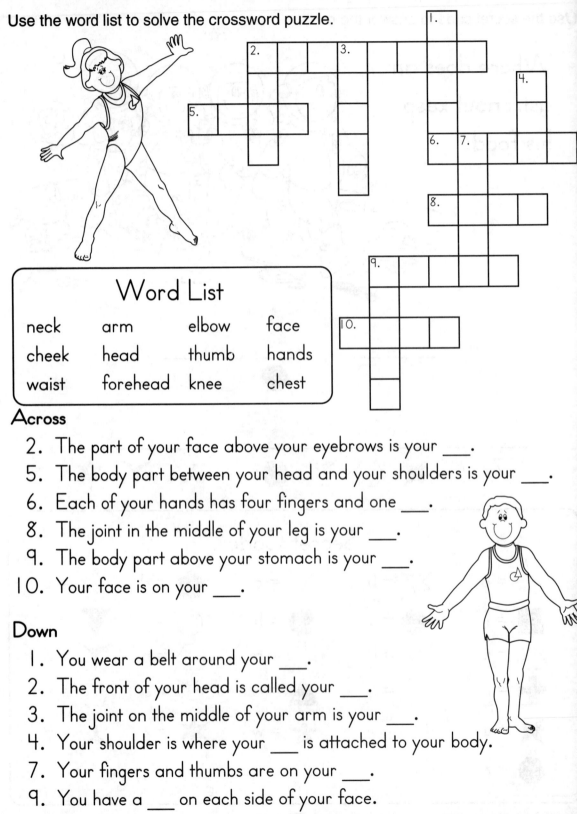

Word List

neck	arm	elbow	face
cheek	head	thumb	hands
waist	forehead	knee	chest

Across
2. The part of your face above your eyebrows is your ___.
5. The body part between your head and your shoulders is your ___.
6. Each of your hands has four fingers and one ___.
8. The joint in the middle of your leg is your ___.
9. The body part above your stomach is your ___.
10. Your face is on your ___.

Down
1. You wear a belt around your ___.
2. The front of your head is called your ___.
3. The joint on the middle of your arm is your ___.
4. Your shoulder is where your ___ is attached to your body.
7. Your fingers and thumbs are on your ___.
9. You have a ___ on each side of your face.

Use the secret code to answer the riddle.

What do you use to keep a rabbit in place?

$\overline{\hspace{0.6cm}}$ $\overline{\hspace{0.6cm}}$ $\overline{\hspace{0.6cm}}$ $\overline{\hspace{0.6cm}}$ $\overline{\hspace{0.6cm}}$ $\overline{\hspace{0.6cm}}$ $\overline{\hspace{0.6cm}}$ $\overline{\hspace{0.6cm}}$ $\overline{\hspace{0.6cm}}$

　3　21　75　15　　　51　33　75　21　69

Secret Code

21 = a	6 = b	45 = c	39 = d	15 = e
9 = f	27 = g	3 = h	66 = i	54 = j
48 = k	57 = l	36 = m	78 = n	72 = o
33 = p	12 = q	75 = r	51 = s	30 = t
42 = u	63 = v	24 = w	60 = x	69 = y
18 = z				

Use the word list to solve the crossword puzzle.

Word List

flying   ticket

runway   travel

pilot   engine

wing   airport

passenger   cockpit

wheels   propeller

Across

1. When you fly on an airplane, you _____ from one place to another.

3. The part of the plane where the pilot sits is the ___.

4. A small airplane might have a _____ to make it fly.

5. A person who rides on a plane is a _____.

9. A long _____ is attached to each side of an airplane.

10. An airplane is _____ when it is in the air.

Down

1. A person buys a _____ to fly on a plane.

2. An airplane uses its _____ to land on the ground.

4. The ___ flys the plane.

6. When travelling by plane, you need to go to an _____.

7. The motor on an airplane is called an _____.

8. The path that airplanes use to take off is called a _____.

Use the secret code to answer the riddle.

What does a flamingo do when it stands on one foot?

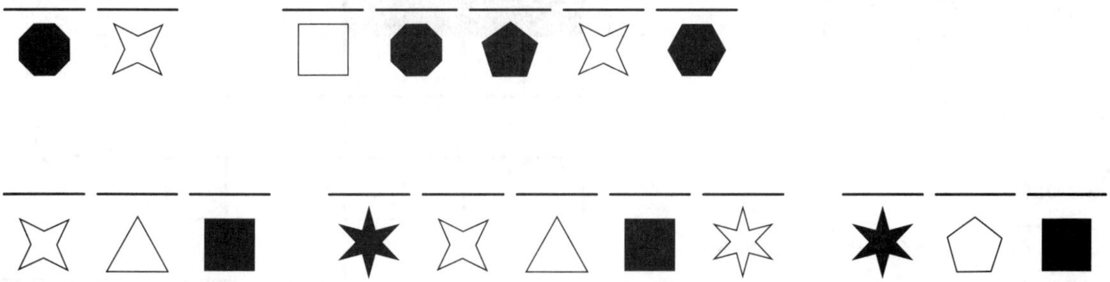

Secret Code

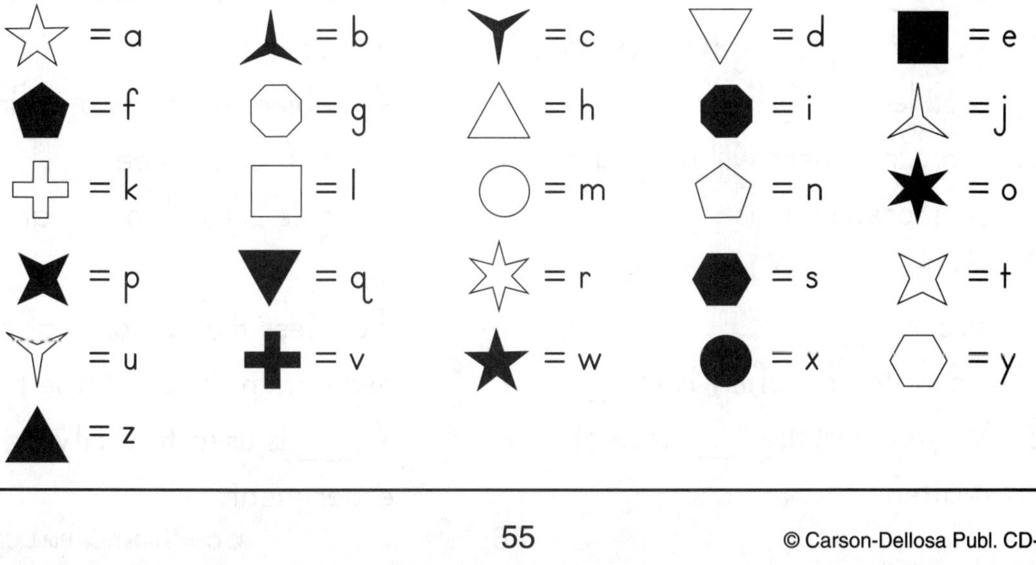

☆ = a	= b	Y = c	▽ = d	■ = e
⬟ = f	⬡ = g	△ = h	⬢(i) = i	= j
✚(k) = k	□ = l	○ = m	⬠ = n	★ = o
✦ = p	▼ = q	✵ = r	⬣ = s	✕ = t
�367 = u	➕ = v	★ = w	● = x	⬡ = y
▲ = z				

Use the word list to solve the crossword puzzle.

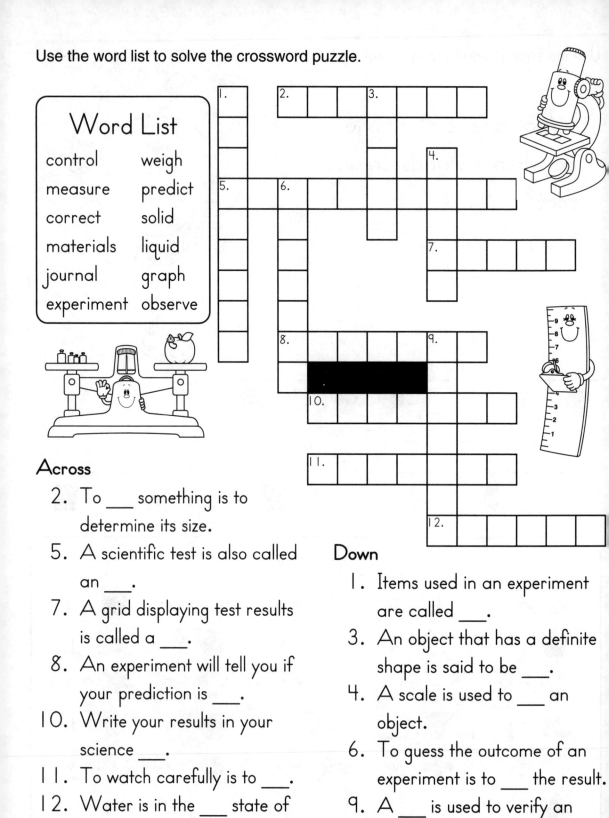

Word List

control	weigh
measure	predict
correct	solid
materials	liquid
journal	graph
experiment	observe

Across

2. To ___ something is to determine its size.
5. A scientific test is also called an ___.
7. A grid displaying test results is called a ___.
8. An experiment will tell you if your prediction is ___.
10. Write your results in your science ___.
11. To watch carefully is to ___.
12. Water is in the ___ state of matter.

Down

1. Items used in an experiment are called ___.
3. An object that has a definite shape is said to be ___.
4. A scale is used to ___ an object.
6. To guess the outcome of an experiment is to ___ the result.
9. A ___ is used to verify an experiment.

Use the secret code to answer the riddle.

What sheet can't be folded?

$\overline{}_{8} \quad \overline{}_{40} \ \overline{}_{92} \ \overline{}_{32} \ \overline{}_{32} \ \overline{}_{28} \quad \overline{}_{96} \ \overline{}_{64} \quad \overline{}_{20} \ \overline{}_{16} \ \overline{}_{32}$

8   40 92 32 32 28   96 64   20 16 32

Secret Code

8 = a	68 = b	16 = c	48 = d	32 = e
64 = f	4 = g	92 = h	20 = i	60 = j
12 = k	84 = l	44 = m	80 = n	96 = o
52 = p	36 = q	72 = r	40 = s	28 = t
88 = u	100 = v	24 = w	56 = x	76 = y
104 = z				

Use the word list to solve the crossword puzzle.

Word List

campground	tent
backpack	shelter
campfire	outdoors
hiking	nature
blanket	forest

Across

1. A bag with shoulder straps used by hikers is a ___.
2. A park where people can put their tents is called a ___.
4. Walking through the woods is called ___.
6. Campers sleep inside a ___.
7. A wooded area is called a ___.
8. Roast marshmallows over a ___.
10. Hikers need to find a ___ during a storm.

Down

1. A heavy ___ will keep you warm.
3. Camping is a fun way to enjoy the ___.
5. Animals, insects, and trees are all part of ___.

Use the secret code to answer the riddle.

Why did the bird fly south?

IT WAS TOO FAR TO WALK

Secret Code

✚ = a	▼ = b	⅄ = c	☆ = d	⬠ = e
✶ = f	Y = g	△ = h	● = i	▢ = j
★ = k	☆ = l	✛ = m	⬠ = n	⅄ = o
⬡ = p	✖ = q	▲ = r	⬢ = s	⬣ = t
■ = u	⬣ = v	Y = w	✶ = x	○ = y
▽ = z				

Use the word list to solve the crossword puzzle.

Word List

habitat	animals	zookeeper	feed	sleep
baby	elephant	snake	ape	zebra

Across

1. A ___ is a reptile that has no arms or legs.
3. The person who cares for the animals at a zoo is the ___.
5. A monkey is sometimes called an ___.
6. Zookeepers ___ small fish to the penguins.
8. A zoo is a good place to go to see many different types of ___.

Down

1. Animals, such as bats, that ___ during the day are called nocturnal.
2. Plants and trees are often used to recreate an animal's natural ___.
3. The ___ is related to the horse and has black and white stripes.
4. An ___ is a large animal with a long trunk.
7. Visitors at the zoo are always excited when a ___ animal is born.